God Is
an Amateur

John R. Claypool

Forward Movement Publications
Cincinnati, Ohio

The Rev. John R. Claypool is rector of St. Luke's Church, Birmingham, Alabama. Chapters in this book were adapted from broadcasts of the Protestant Hour in the fall of 1988, presented under the direction of the Episcopal Radio-TV Foundation, Inc.

© 1994, Forward Movement Publications
412 Sycamore Street, Cincinnati, Ohio 45202 USA

It is time to gather up what
we know and believe and hope
and pass it on
to those coming after us.

I do this lovingly for
my children

Rowan and Anne,
C.T. and Amy,
Laura

and my grandchildren
Cate, John Rowan, and Ashley

Acknowledgments

Nothing is ever done exclusively by a lone individual, and volumes of this sort are truly corporate in their origins. An appropriate sense of gratitude necessitates the mention of these co-creators of the words that follow:

The Rev. Louis J. Scheuddig of the Episcopal Radio-TV Foundation, whose invitation initiated this process;

Marjorie Swanson, my secretary and partner in ministry, who typed and retyped these words with unfailing skill and good spirit;

The Rev. Robert Horine, editor with Forward Movement Publications;

Ann S. Claypool, my beloved wife, who supports me patiently by the gift of her love;

All the persons—remembered and forgotten—whose wisdom enlightened me and whose sharing of themselves and their lives have enriched my story.

John R. Claypool

Contents

Introduction

My first contact with the radio program called "The National Protestant Hour" was a very memorable one. I was driving along one Sunday morning in the middle 1950s and in moving the dial from station to station caught the sound of a cultivated voice and decided to listen further. The longer this one spoke, the more impressed I became. I remember thinking: "Here is someone who really knows what he is talking about. I have never heard anyone who seems more 'sure footed' in the way he handles the Christian gospel." Needless to say, I was curious as to who this was and what kind of program this might be, and at the end, the preacher was identified as the Rev. Samuel Shoemaker of Pittsburgh, and the program "The National Protestant Hour." From that day forward, I listened to it regularly wherever I went and over the years heard many of the great pulpit giants of both this country and Great Britain.

Imagine, then, the flood of feelings that I experienced when in the spring of 1988 the Rev. Skip Scheuddig of the Episcopal Radio-Television Foundation called and invited me to become a participant! It was one of those things that frankly I had never even dreamed of doing, which made the opportunity that much more gracious.

What I decided to do was select twelve basic points which I felt were of genuine significance. I was once asked to address the question: "If I Had But One Last Sermon To Preach," and invited to share *the* best truth I knew. I followed something of that same approach in settling on the sermons for this volume. They do not represent all the Christian vision by any means, but certain important facets of it that have nurtured and inspired me and hopefully will do the same for you.

The actual series was broadcast beginning on September 4, 1988, and concluding on November 2, 1988. Three of the sermons focused on specific seasons—Labor Day, All Saints Day, and Thanksgiving Day. The rest were truths applicable for all seasons.

It was a personal joy to be able to give back to a tradition that across the years had given so much to me. I hope this different form of giving will assume a life of its own and be caught up by the One whose will it is to bless, and used as only the Holy One knows best.

John R. Claypool
February 1994

Amateurism, God, and Ourselves

Genesis 1

Words are like little children. They are always in motion and almost never still for long. For example, back in 1675, just nine years after the terrible London fire had devastated so much of that city, Sir Christopher Wren laid the cornerstone of what was to be his most ambitious undertaking—the rebuilding of St. Paul's Cathedral. He worked on the project for over thirty-five years, and the experts say he poured more of his genius into this edifice than any other building he ever designed. When the project was finally completed, and Sir Christopher himself was a very old man, he personally conducted the then reigning monarch, Queen Anne, on an extensive tour through the whole building. When it was over, he waited with bated breath for her reactions. In typical British terseness, she used three adjectives to sum up her feelings: "It is awful, it is artificial, it is amusing." Can you imagine how the old builder must have felt when the one person whose opinion he valued the most described the "magnum opus" of his life in this way?

However, a biographer says that on hearing these words, Sir Christopher let out an audible sigh of relief, sank to his knees, and thanked her majesty for her graciousness. How could such a reaction be possible? Words are always in motion and never stand still. For you see, back in 1710, the word "awful" meant "awe-inspiring," the word "artificial" meant "artistic," and the word "amusing" meant "amazing."

Words like little children are always changing, which is why, incidentally, we have to keep on retranslating our scriptures and reformulating our liturgies, because words like everything else participate in an existence where the only thing that does not change is the fact of change itself.

And what has happened to words like "awful" and "artificial" and "amusing" has also happened to another English word, the term "amateur." As we use it in today's parlance, it stands for a person of limited competence. An "amateur" is the opposite of a professional, and carries the implication of a person who does not do something with much skill and may even be something of a bumbler. However, this was not the case originally. Our English word "amateur" comes from the Latin root *amare,* which is the verb for "love." In its original intent, an "amateur" was a person who did whatever she or he did "for the love of it;" that is, their motivation came from within and not from without. An "amateur" was not paid to do something, nor coerced by any external force. The reason for such a person's act was positive intentionality. Here were folk who did what they did for the sheer joy of it.

In its original sense then, one could go so far as to describe God as an "amateur"; in fact, this is precisely the import of the first chapter of Genesis. If you read those lyric lines as the inspired poetry they were meant to be, the image comes through of a Mystery who has life and is desirous to share that life with others. You can almost hear God saying to God's self: "This aliveness that I'm enjoying, this wonderful power to be and to do—it is simply too good to keep to myself. I want others to taste something of this ecstasy. I want the delight of aliveness to be a shared experience."

Therefore, we watch in Genesis as this primal Generosity begins to act. Out of all the things God could have done, the Holy One freely decides to create. There is no hint of coercion or external motivation here. Next, this One proceeds to carry out skillfully this intention to share, and the whole process comes to a climax in the refrain that echoes throughout the whole chapter: "And God looked on what God had created and said, 'It is good, it is good, it is very, very good.'"

The Hebrew image here is that of a little child having constructed something and then bringing in another to view it. Jumping up and down with delight, rubbing his hands together excitedly, he exclaims: "Isn't it grand? Isn't it wonderful? Look what I have brought into being!" All of this, of course, is precisely what lies behind the original meaning of this word amateur. Here is One who freely selects an option out of all of the possibilities, who effectively brings that potentiality into being, and then finds abundant delight in reflecting on the whole process.

In our modern usage, to call God an amateur might sound like a slight, but in the original sense of the word, it gives us a glimpse into the very heart of the Eternal and helps us see that everything that exists in our world goes back to a Generosity that acted as it did for the sheer joy of it.

And this particular vision of God has practical relevance for each one of us, because the same book of Genesis goes on to affirm that we humans are made in the image of that Great Amateur; that is, we come to the fullness of our potential when we understand ourselves as having the same capacity to choose freely among many options, to act creatively on something that we want to do, and then experience the delight that comes from doing life in this way. The possibility of being an amateur is within the reach of everyone of us, and this represents the best image I know of what it is we were meant to be.

For many people, I am afraid, the idea of their labor being that of an amateur is rather far-fetched. There are many who feel the only possibility for this kind of experience lies outside their work. Their hobbies and avocations may have the characteristics of amateurism, but not the thing they do to make their livelihood. I do not want to be naive here. At the same time, I raise the possibility that if we were daring and imaginative enough and really believed that being an amateur is the essence of our true identity, there are ways of asking ourselves, "What do I really want to do? What are my best characteristics? What brings me the greatest delight of soul?" and then begin to search for a way to make even our labor an expression of true amateurism. It may take lots of risk-taking, but the possibility of being what God is exists for every one of us.

There is a wonderful old story about a Jewish man named Isaac who was the son of one named Yeckel. His family had lived for generations in Cracow, Poland, and they had always been very poor. Isaac kept having a vivid dream. It took place in Prague, Czechoslovakia. Isaac was told if he would dig at a certain place under a bridge, he would find there immense treasure that would make him rich for the rest of his life. Finally, to the great dismay of his more practical family members, he announced that he was going to journey to Prague to test the reality of this beckoning. His contemporaries thought him crazy, but he set out nonetheless.

He worked his way carefully across the center of Europe and finally reached Prague, where he had never been before, only to find it exactly as he had visualized it in his dreams. He went right to the bridge under which he was to dig and with great excitement began to excavate. Suddenly, however, he felt a hand on his shoulder. It was a policeman saying, "This is public property. You are defacing it. You are under arrest." He was taken to a police station, where an inspector began to interrogate him. Poor Isaac was so frightened that he did not know what to do but tell the truth about his dream. With that, the inspector laid back his head and laughed, and said, "You foolish dreamer. Don't you know there is nothing to these night fantasies?" He said, "Why, I myself have been having a dream of late. It was that if I would go to a village in Poland called Cracow, wherever that is, and go to the house of one Isaac, son of Yeckel, whoever that might be, and go into his kitchen and dig under

13

his stove, there I would find a treasure to make me rich for the rest of my life. But would I not look foolish if I were to leave my good job here and go way off to Poland on such a wild goose chase?"

With that, he cuffed Isaac across the cheek and said, "Grow up, foolish dreamer, become a man, do something practical," and proceeded to throw him out of the police station. But Isaac, although harshly treated, was by no means depressed. He made his way back to Cracow, went to his own house and into his own kitchen, dug under his own stove and there found the treasure that did in fact make him rich!

It is an old motif actually, the idea that sometimes you have to go halfway around the world before you finally discover what is resident in your own situation. But here is the hope that if we will listen carefully to our dreams, pay attention to the beckonings of our own hearts, and heed things that draw us for the sheer love of it, such things can become the golden thread that leads to our deepest and highest identity. We are made in the image of an "Amateur," a God who did what God did for the love of it. Please, for God's sake and your own, do not abandon the hope that you can become one too!

And Yet

Luke 8:26-39

Several years ago now, I found myself in an exceedingly painful place. The Psalmist calls it "the valley of the shadow of death." My ten-year-old daughter had just died of leukemia. The last months of her life had been filled with excruciating and unbelievable pain, and after it was all over, I found myself in a twilight zone of despair and dismay. At that juncture, a wise old friend said to me one afternoon: "I know it does not feel like it now, but I want you to realize that every profound experience of change has two sides to it. There is, of course, the loss dimension, having to give up something you once highly prized. But there is also a gain dimension. In every change, you get something you did not have before. Some burden is taken off you. Certain energies which were devoted to one cause are now freed up to be invested elsewhere. There is a relief dimension to every loss, and the key is learning to deal honestly with both sides of the change phenomenon. It would be unhealthy to deny the loss dimension. It is there and must somehow be appropriated. However, it is just as unhealthy to ignore the gain dimension, and the new possibilities that are now available to you."

My friend was right about the distance between such words and my feelings at that moment. I was much too engulfed in my grief to be able to hear this concept. In fact, my first impression was a feeling of real anger, a sense that this one really did not understand and was trying to "paper over my pain" for his own benefit. However, several weeks after our conversation, something happened that enabled me to begin to catch a glimpse of what he was saying. My wife, my son, and I went one night to a little fish restaurant in Louisville, Kentucky, where the four of us had often gone before my daughter had gotten sick. As we sat down in that familiar setting, somehow my eyes fell on the empty chair that was now a part of our family circle, and the sense of irreparable loss that it represented was almost more than my psyche could bear. What that unoccupied chair represented for the future was more painful than any physical discomfort. But then my focus shifted to the chair across from me, where my then twelve-year-old son was seated. He looked so small and frail in that moment, and I realized how little power I had to protect him or anyone in so mysterious a universe. But then, all of a sudden it dawned on me: "For all you have lost, there is still a great deal left. If you give up in the face of this grief, and say in effect, 'Stop the world, I want to get off,' what that will say to your son is that he is of no value and his sister was all that mattered."

I quickly realized that my heart had more places in it than the one my beloved daughter had occupied. There was still an ocean of affection for my surviving child. That was the moment it came clear to me that either I could spend the rest of my life focusing on what I had lost, or I could begin to recognize what my old friend had pointed out; namely, that there was a gain dimension in the valley of the shadow of grief as well. I now had more time and more money to invest in one child than I had had with the responsibility of two. It was not a choice that I would ever have made, but since it had been made for me, I still had a measure of freedom, which was how I would respond.

That was the night I decided to live again and to focus on what was left and the kind of future that was still possible, rather than on what was gone and could never be retrieved out of an unalterable past. It is the decision every grieving person has to make at some time or the other. Will we choose to turn our faces to the future and the possibilities of meaning that are still to be found there, or will we fixate our attention on the past and live forever in the land of memory and nostalgia and regret?

This is the shape of the freedom that has been given to us humans. It is a genuine thing, but by no means absolute. I am certainly not free always to determine what will happen to me circumstantially, but I am free to determine how I will respond to what happens, which is why I said that every grieving person gets to a point in their processing of loss where they side either with what is coming in terms of open possibilities, or with what is gone beyond all reach of living relationship.

We have all known people who chose to let the death of a significant other mark the end of their own meaningful existence. A Bible story describes just such a person. Jesus had crossed the Sea of Galilee in the hope of getting some rest. No sooner had he landed in a sparsely populated region known as Gadara than he was met by a pathetic character who was utterly deranged and out of touch with his senses. He had no clothes on. By day and by night, he slashed himself with stones. Interestingly enough, he made his home in a cemetery. Myron Madden has offered the suggestion that here was a person who had not been able to come to terms with some grief that had occurred in his life. He had come to the place where the dead were buried, and he could not get out of the graveyard! What he had lost was so overwhelming that he could not even glimpse what was left or the meaning that might be made of the opportunities that were still available to him. This person is a stark reminder of what grief can do to any one of us.

The perspective that my old friend offered me that day is quite relevant when it comes to recovery from grief. Focusing only on the losses that change brings into our lives is leaving out an important aspect of reality. There is also a gain dimension as well. The question becomes: on which of these will we focus?

The New Testament contains a glowing example of someone who chose what was left and stands in contrast to the man Jesus encountered in Gadara. I am thinking now about Paul the apostle, and specifically about many of the letters he wrote that are now part of our New Testament canon. As you may know, a great portion of these were written while Paul was imprisoned in a variety of places. Finding himself in jail must have been a very embarrassing and frustrating experience for someone as energetic and as law-abiding as the great apostle. He easily could have allowed this kind of change in his circumstances to have embittered him or crushed him into disabling despair. However, he recognized the presence of a gain-dimension in all of this, and therefore chose to use these periods of forced inactivity to shift gears, to reflect on what he was doing, and to write important messages to the young churches he had so recently brought into being.

Someone has observed that had it not been for imprisonment, Paul might never have taken the time to write down these priceless words, for he was at heart an activist and a missionary. Yet a significant portion of our present New Testament is a living symbol of how loss can be approached creatively and hopefully, and how one can stoop to pick up the pieces of what change has broken and set about to see what can be made of what is left.

That old friend, who spoke to me so honestly years ago, ended his conversation with me by saying, "The two most important words to remember in the face of devastating change are the words, 'and yet.'" It is essential to look tragedy in the face and not evade or avoid any of the painful losses that make up that experience. But having been honest with that side of things, then to say "and yet" is the way out and the way through. These two little words really do hold the secret. They sum up what I did that night in the little fish restaurant when I shifted my gaze from the empty chair to the child that was still alive and said to myself, "I have lost a daughter, *and yet* there is still a son, there is still work to do, there is still my own life to live out and to fulfill. I choose to side with the 'and yet.'"

This is exactly what Saint Paul did when he found himself in prison. You see, no matter what your circumstance, the possibility of saying "and yet" is open to us all. Change brings two things in its wake— a loss of some of the things we did have and the gain of opportunities that were never ours before. With this awareness, may God help us to embrace what is still possible, and therefore make our way creatively, not just *into* the valley of the shadow of change, but *through* that valley to the light that is always on the other side!

So let it be, O God, so let it be!

Love and Creativity

Luke 19:1-9

G.K. Chesterton once observed that many of the most familiar fairy tales could only have been written in a Christian context. While they do not use specifically religious images, the messages they convey often grow straight out of the Christian vision of reality.

Take, for example, that wonderful story called "Beauty and the Beast." You may remember that a poor man had nothing with which to feed his family, and in desperation one night, he climbed over the wall of a nearby castle and was stealing some fruit when he was caught by the owner, a grotesque figure called Beast. He had the head of an animal, the torso of a man, and was horror personified to look upon. Beast told the poor man that he had only two options: he could rot away as a prisoner in the castle dungeon, or he could go home and tell his youngest daughter, named Beauty, that she must come and live with him in the castle.

The poor man went home with a heavy heart, and when he explained his plight, Beauty immediately said, "Of course I will go to the castle. Anything to save you from such an awful fate." And so she went, whereupon Beast told her that he had loved her from afar for years and wanted very much to marry her and make her the first lady of the whole castle. However, he was so grotesque in appearance that Beauty could not bring herself to agree to such intimacy, and so she politely declined.

As the days went by, Beast continued to propose his love and Beauty continued to refuse. With all of that Beast grew sadder and sadder, and then suddenly one day something shifted in Beauty's heart. A love she had not known before sprang up like a flame, and to Beast's amazement she announced that she would, in fact, marry him and give him the gift of her love. With that, she leaned over and kissed his grotesque face, and the moment that happened, Beast turned into a shining prince. He then related how he had been placed under an evil spell by a wicked witch and was doomed to remain grotesque in form until someone loved him in spite of how he appeared.

Here, I would contend, is a distinctly Christian message—that love is not just a response to loveliness, but is also the power to create loveliness where it did not exist before. If we reserve our affection for people and situations that already have beauty, we are not exercising the power of love in all its fullness. What Beauty did for Beast is not only possible, but perhaps the most needed single thing in our broken, troubled world.

If you look at the ministry of Jesus of Nazareth, does it not come clear that he understood love in a creative as well as a responsive sense? He became known at the very outset as "a friend of sinners," and this was a great dismay to the folk who only saw love as something you do in relation to the already lovely. But Jesus did not so restrict his affection. There is a moving story in the nineteenth chapter of Luke about our Lord entering the city of Jericho toward the end of his ministry. By then his reputation had become widespread, so people lined the streets to catch a glimpse of this wonder-working rabbi. Perhaps the most despised of all the citizens in that town was a man named Zacchaeus. He was Jew by birth, but he had chosen to do a very dastardly thing; he had gone to work for the occupation forces of the Roman Empire. Jews who did this were looked on as real turncoats, exploiting their own people in the service of an enemy.

One cannot help but wonder what caused Zacchaeus to turn so against his own kinfolks. One possible clue lies in a tiny detail of this story. We are told that Zacchaeus had to climb up into a tree in order to see Jesus because he was "small of stature." Could it be that, growing up, Zacchaeus had been ridiculed by his contemporaries for something that was not his fault at all? None of us wills the height to which we ultimately grow. It is part of the mysterious "given" of our existence. How cruel it is to make fun of folk for something over which they have no control. It could be that this wound of cruelty was allowed to fester and infected the whole outlook of this individual. Perhaps becoming a Roman tax collector was Zacchaeus' way of getting back at those who had originally caused him pain. No one can be sure, of course, but the net result is that here was a really despised and unlovable human being.

And what did Jesus do? Because he realized that love had the power to create loveliness rather than just respond to loveliness, he shocked all Jericho that day by stopping under the tree and saying simply, "Zacchaeus, come down, I would love to have dinner at your house." It was probably the first time in years that anyone had spoken cordially to this individual, much less implied that they would like to have the pleasure of his company. Jesus did for Zacchaeus what Beauty did for Beast; that is, he offered his love as a gift, and the same creative impact resulted from this action. Although we are not told exactly what transpired around the table, Zacchaeus emerged from this encounter with Jesus a genuinely transformed individual. He said, "I now voluntarily promise not to exact more than is appropriate for taxes, and a great portion of what I have already acquired, I am going to devote to genuinely humane causes." A beast of a person was turned into a prince of kindness because love has the power to create loveliness where it did not exist before. We do not have to wait for people to become lovable in order to love them. Our actions of love have the power to bring such a reality into existence.

This is why, of course, Jesus dared to say on another occasion, "You have always heard it said, you are to love your neighbor or the person who is already lovable, but I call you to something higher: to love your enemies, to do good to those who despise you, and to pray for those who may be persecuting you." This is the way we do become part of the answer and not part of the problem. I had a wise old cousin say to me one night, "You know, the people who are the most unlovable are actually the most in need of love, and are least likely to get it, because their behavior turns people in the opposite direction." I have never forgotten the wisdom of that insight, and I try to remind myself, in the face of the genuinely unlovable, that here are folk who at a deeper level are crying out for the very thing they are systematically destroying. The most unlovable *are* the most in need of love, but unless we realize the creative potential of love, we will miss a golden opportunity to inject something very different into a poisoned situation.

I heard once about a young man of genuine Christian maturity who was drafted into the military and took with him his lifestyle of kindness and piety. The old sergeant who was in charge of boot training was offended by the obvious goodness in this young man. Therefore, he set out in every way possible to break down his character and to reduce him to a lower level of functioning. He was abusive in the way he spoke to the lad, unfair in what he asked of him. In fact, by every means possible he attempted to crush his spirit, but through it all the young man responded in unfailing goodwill. Late one Saturday night, after having too much to drink, the sergeant happened to come through the barracks and saw this young man kneeling in prayer by his bunk. The sight set off the worst in the old sergeant. He began to make fun of the young man in loud and abusive tones, but this one did not budge from his posture on his knees. When unable to rile him verbally, the sergeant sat down on one of the bunks, took off one of his muddy boots, and from

25

across the room heaved it at the lad. It hit him in the temple, stunned him for a moment, but then he resumed his prayerful posture. When that failed, the sergeant took off the other boot and flung it equally as hard. Once again, it struck the lad, but he refused to flare back. With a parting round of oaths, the sergeant stumbled on to his quarters and went to bed.

The next morning, when the sergeant awoke, the first thing he saw were his muddy boots—cleaned, polished, and sitting neatly by his bed. It was more than the sergeant could tolerate. He went and found the lad and said, "What is it with you? I have done everything in my power to drag you down, and you continue to respond as you do. What is the secret of your humaneness?" This was the beginning, not of a young Christian being reduced to inhumanity, but of a less-than-mature person being called up to possibilities within himself he had never realized before. You see, love is not just a response to the already lovely; it is a power than can create loveliness where it did not exist before. The whole thrust of the Christian religion is an invitation to love in this transforming way.

Come, then, my beauties, in the name of Christ, it is time to kiss the beasts!

Choose Your Pain

Mark 8:31-35

Some things sound so true the first time you hear them, so wise and practical and down-to-earth. Take, for example, the song Simon and Garfunkle made famous back in 1969. It was called "I Am A Rock." You may remember it. The singer has built barriers to keep others at a distance because friendship and love involve the risk of pain.

The first time I heard the song it sounded very authentic, for who of us has not gone through an experience of this sort and made the resolve to react in this same way? You open yourself up to another person in love and vulnerability and what happens? You get hurt in the process. Either that one betrays you or manipulates you or disappoints and in some way violates you. The tenderest part of your being is slashed to shreds, and you react by saying: "All right, if this is what comes of loving, I will not run this risk again. I will not set myself up for this kind of pain. I will go it alone, build a barricade around myself, become an island, a rock. Then I will not have to suffer." This is a very common reaction to one of life's most basic experiences, which is why, I suppose, that record became so popular.

However, with the passage of time and as a result of some genuine reflection, I find myself wondering if these words are really as wise as they sounded on first hearing. Sometimes when you take a second look at something, it assumes a different shape, and this is what has happened to me as I have pondered the relation between the reality of pain and the acts of loving and not loving.

Now to be sure, no one can deny the fact that when we enter into a loving relationship with another person, we open ourselves to the possibility of suffering. This thing called love, by its very nature, involves getting close and establishing intimacy. This does make us highly vulnerable to what the other does or fails to do. However, does it automatically follow that by choosing not to love, one is assured of never having to suffer?

This is the part of the argument that I find to be highly questionable. What would you think of a person who responded to an acute attack of food poisoning by saying, "Look, I have had it with eating! It was ingesting all that food which caused me this agony. I will never subject myself to that possibility again. As of this moment, I give up eating forever!" Now, of course you could say of such a person that their solution is correct in a very narrow sense. After all, if one never eats, one will never experience food poisoning. But in the larger framework of human existence, such a strategy is simply unworkable. Given our physical make-up, avoiding the pains of food poisoning by not eating simply opens us up to a whole new range of pains; namely, the pain of hunger and malnutrition and eventually starving to death. As real as the risk of eating may be, it in fact holds more positive promise than the way of not eating. There are certain "cures," it turns out, that are worse than the disease itself.

Now, I acknowledge there is an element of the ludicrous in this particular analogy, yet the principle of personal survival is not that much different than the principle of bodily survival. Think about it. We humans need relationships with other human beings in order to become human and stay human. This is just as crucial to our humanness as the need of food is for our bodies, which is why the song is profoundly incorrect when it says, "If I had never loved, I never would have cried."

To be sure, one would never have cried the tears of disappointment or violation, but what about the tears of loneliness and isolation and cut-offness? This is pain, too, and from a human standpoint, something just as agonizing as the pain of betrayal. Here is a reality that one has to take seriously the moment one makes the decision not to love. Father Joseph Gallenger of Baltimore is right to the point, it seems to me, in saying, "Our human choice is never between pain and no pain, but rather between the pain of loving and the pain of not loving." I consider these very wise words indeed, and they need to be set over against the words of this song as a better way of understanding the relation of pain and the processes of loving and not loving.

It seems to me there are two implications here of tremendous importance. The first is the recognition that pain is an inevitable part of life, no matter how we go about living it. Therefore, it is futile to attempt to escape pain altogether. I realize there is no desire embedded any deeper in our human make-up than the desire not to suffer. Yet, when this becomes one's only goal in life, it invariably leads to disappointment. No matter which way you turn, the risk of pain is there, and the quicker we disabuse ourselves of the fantasy that somehow we can avoid suffering, the better we will be.

I think this was the truth Jesus was stating one day when he acknowledged to his companions that his pattern of loving sinners had put him on collision course with the religious establishment of his day. As a result of all this, he predicted that he was going to have to suffer many things at the hands of his enemies. However, he was not in despair at such a prospect. This is what he had been sent into the world to do, and he was firmly convinced that some good would come out of it. On hearing this, Simon Peter took Jesus aside and remonstrated with him, saying vigorously: "There ought to be a way for you to accomplish your mission without having to suffer." Jesus responded almost vehemently by saying, "Get behind me, Satan! You are not speaking the words of God, but the words of the Evil One."

I think Jesus regarded the idea that there is a way to live life authentically without ever having to suffer as a dangerous fantasy by which we must not be seduced. He realized that if one spent one's whole life trying to avoid suffering, this would simply bring even greater suffering into one's experience. Father

Gallenger is right. "Our human choice is never be-tween pain and no pain." That option simply is not open. It never has been, nor will it ever be. No matter how one lives, some pain is inevitable.

Therefore, the choice becomes: which kind of pain will it be? Will it be the kind of suffering that goes with loving, making one's self vulnerable to another, or will it be the form of suffering that comes from not loving—that special kind of agony that grows out of isolation and aloneness and cut-offness? This is the second implication that I find in Father Gallenger's words. They close off a false option and set before us a truly promising one.

The fact of the matter is that there is no fulfill-ment possible down the road of not loving. It violates the very essence of our beings as creatures of related-ness. I came into this world through the loving action of two other people. I could not have learned to speak or make my way very far into this world without the gift that connectedness with others brings. There-fore, to try to become human and remain human by never loving at all is an utter contradiction of our very natures.

Think about it. The worst punishment we have devised, short of death, is the punishment of solitary confinement, because this cuts us off from the very thing we have to have in order to come to human fulfillment. It is not surprising to me that the song writer uses the images of a "rock" and "an island" as the logical end of the way of not loving, because in effect, we do revert to the inanimate when we give up our willingness to love. It brings a kind of pain to the essence of our being that is even worse, I believe, than the pain of disappointment and   betrayal.

C.S. Lewis tells about waking up in the middle of the night years ago, and not being able to go back to sleep. He was living alone at the time; and as he lay there in utter darkness, with nothing to see, nothing to hear, and with no one to whom to relate, it dawned on him that such a condition was the utter antithesis of what it meant to be a vibrant human being. Then the thought struck him, "What if I had to live on in this kind of vacuum forever?" Such a prospect appeared more fearful than a thousand burning hells. Then he realized that this kind of aloneness was the logical end of not loving or of refusing to relate. Could it be, he wondered, that we will get in eternity exactly what we lived for in time—no more and no less? This means that if we have loved, the chance to live on in related-ness and to grow by giving and receiving from others will increase. However, if we chose not to love, all we get is ourselves—lonely, isolated rocks and islands. What could be worse, really, than being forever and utterly and totally alone? You talk about pain and agony; this would be the worst imaginable!

Therefore, I think it is clear, that although the risk of pain is very real down the road of loving, at least this offers the possibility of genuine fulfillment, and I ask you, are not good odds finally better than no odds at all? I think so. Jesus says in our text that "the one who tries to save his life will lose it, but the one who is willing to lose his life will find it." I believe he is suggesting here that when we try to save our lives by avoiding suffering through not loving, what we really wind up losing is our own true selves. On the other hand, the willingness to risk hurt, the daring to lose one's self in an act of connecting up with another, holds the secret of what we humans need to do in order to be fulfilled.

I come back, then, to a song that sounded so wise on first hearing. Someone decides to love, it does not turn out well, and so the person resolves never to love again. It is an understandable response, but in the long run, a tragic one. The deeper truth is this: we humans are never given a choice between pain and no pain, but rather between the pain of loving and the pain of not loving. Either way you go, there is a risk, but down one road there lies nothing but loneliness and cut-offness; down the other, for all its fateful possibilities, there is at least a chance of genuine fulfillment. I repeat, are not good odds better than no odds at all? Come then, with courage, let us resolve to love.

Hearing the Voice of God

Exodus 3:1-6

The Bible is filled with stories of God actually speaking to human beings. A good example is the scripture at the beginning of this chapter, where Moses found himself confronted directly by the Holy One and having very specific things said to him about what he was to do and where he was to go in the future. I have always been intrigued by such stories, but also a bit dismayed, for in all of my sixty-one years now, no such direct form of audible communication has ever occurred in my experience. I would have loved for God to have materialized before my eyes on occasion, or spoken in sounds that would have fallen audibly on my ears. However, to be perfectly honest, although I have hungered for such direct encounters with the Almighty, I have never been addressed in the form that is so often described in the pages of Holy Scripture.

Then several years ago, I had an experience that helped enlarge my understanding of this whole business of how the Divine One communicates with humankind. I had become deeply involved in the life of a man who was a member of a parish I served in Texas. He was a delightful human being, a scientist by training, but a lay theologian in terms of what he had chosen to do with his life. He was a faithful husband and the father of three teenage children. He bore a heavy load of civic responsibility and was an effective leader in the church which I served. I was greatly grieved the day this one was diagnosed as having a very lethal form of cancer, and in a relatively short time, while still in his mid-forties, this good man was taken away in a spasm of indescribable suffering. I happened to be in his room when the final hour came. When I got home that night I could not sleep. I lay awake in the dark hours of the night asking, "Why does there have to be cancer in a world created by a good God? And why, in the face of so many non-productive citizens, was this man not healed, but allowed to die? His wife needed him. His children will be the less for losing contact with him. All of us who knew him have now become badly deprived. Why did this have to happen at this time to such a one?" I thought of all the times I had gone to nursing homes and seen room after room of aged people who had lost all touch with their bodies and their mental faculties, and yet, for some reason they lingered on and on. Here was one in the flower of his usefulness, taken so quickly. I lay there tossing and turning, as I had so often before in the face of those enormous dilemmas and ambiguities that events of tragedy always evoke. The bottom line was that I was genuinely dismayed about the way the universe appeared to be run in relation to this man.

The next morning, when I got to my office, I found on my desk a little paperback book by Hugh Prather, entitled *Notes To Myself*. To this day, I do not know who put this volume there or how it happened to come into the orbit of my consciousness on that particular morning. Rather aimlessly, for I was badly fatigued, I opened the book and my eyes fell on the words which Prather had penned during the illness of his own young wife. Here is what he wrote: "She may die before morning. But I have been with her four years. Four years. There is no way I could feel cheated if I did not have her for another day. I didn't deserve her for one minute, God knows. And I may die before morning. What I must do is to die now. I must accept the justice of death and the injustice of life. I have lived a good life—longer than many, better than most. Tony died when he was twenty. I have had thirty-two years. I couldn't ask for another day. What did I do to deserve birth? It was a gift. I am me—that is a miracle. I had no right to a single minute. Some are given a single hour. And yet I have had thirty-two years. Few can choose when they will die. I choose to accept death now. As of this moment, I give up my 'right to live.' I give up my 'right' to her life. But it's morning. I have been given another day. Another day to hear and read and smell and walk and love and glory. I am alive for another day. I think of those who aren't."[1]

As I put down the book, I was astonished, and it suddenly dawned on me that perhaps *appropriateness* is a better sign of God's speaking to us than mere *audibility*. You see, the words of Hugh Prather, at that particular moment, were precisely what I needed to shift my perspective and gain a better way to handle my grief. I had been so overwhelmed by the intensity of my loss that I had slipped into a spirit of entitlement, almost as if this friend's life was a possession that I deserved, and therefore God was a thief of sorts to take away something that rightly belonged to me. Suddenly, the images of "the justice of death" and "the injustice of life" brought me back to a much more creative perspective, that life is gift, every single particle of it. All the people we love, and the very opportunity to live ourselves, do not come as the result of our having earned or deserved them. They are the gifts of that Generous One we call God. Thus, instead of being filled with anger and all kinds of questions as to why this man had died, it suddenly dawned on me that the more appropriate response was to give thanks that he had ever lived at all and to be grateful for the grace he had been in my life. It turned out that I was in much better shape to minister to that grieving family and to the whole community because of those words that had so mysteriously appeared out of nowhere on my desk.

I would like to suggest that Hugh Prather's book was as direct a communication from God as the bush that burned for Moses and the voice that spoke to him from heaven out there in the desert. The point that I want to make is that we should not limit the reality of God's "speaking" to us to the realm of the audible. I want to add the category of timeliness and appropriateness to this whole phenomenon and suggest that whenever something occurs that fits our need the way a key fits a lock, this too should be regarded as a form of God's "speaking" to us or dealing with us. There is nothing that we can do to make that One love us any more than he already does, nor is there anything we can do to make that One stop loving us. "God knows the way we take," claims the Psalmist. Therefore, we need to open ourselves to the possibility that God can communicate with us in a thousand different ways. If we will make appropriateness a mark of divine communication, rather than something we hear with our ears, it just may come clear that God has been "speaking" to us all along, but we were the ones who failed to recognize it because we were expecting something in a different form.

It is my deepest faith that God both desires and has the ability to make intimate contact with every human creature. After all, St. Augustine claimed that God loves each of us as if there were none other in all the world to love, and that he loves all as he loves each. This being the case, expect the Holy One to do high business with your soul, and begin to look not necessarily for a voice you can hear with your ears, but events that correspond amazingly to the need of that moment. The book that appeared somehow on my desk authentically "spoke" to my situation. Appropriateness, not audibility, is the clue, and if you will widen your understanding to include this form of "speaking," who knows, dear friend, what may become a burning bush for you?

[1] Hugh Prather, *Notes to Myself* (Moab, Utah: Real People Press, 1970), pp. 2-3.

Speaking the Truth In Love

Matthew 7:7-8

There is a disease in our modern culture that is receiving more and more attention in the popular media. It is called "anorexia." Frederick Buechner has had first hand experience with this disorder in his own family and he describes the symptoms in this way: "Nothing for breakfast. A diet soda for lunch. Maybe a little lettuce with low calorie dressing for supper or once in a while, when everybody has gone to bed, a binge on ice cream which you get rid of in the bathroom later. Relentless exercise. Obsession with food, cooking great quantities of it for everybody except yourself. In time you come to look like a victim of Dachau—the sunken eyes and hollow cheeks, the marionette arms and calfless legs . . . If you are told your life itself is in jeopardy, it makes no difference because not even dying is as fearsome as getting fat, a view that the combined industries of fashion, dietetic food, and advertising all endorse. In every respect but this, you may be as sane as everybody else. In this, you are mad as a hatter."[1]

Buechner goes on to say that anorexia sounds like a modern disease, but old phrases like "pining away," or "wasting away" suggest that it may have been around unnamed for a long, long time. Nobody seems to know exactly what it is all about, although there are endless theories. The most common is that young anorexics are trying to strike free of parental control. When the big people say: "Take a bite for Mommy," or "Eat this for Daddy," this is where they decide to draw the battle line. The more desperately these people are urged to eat, the more desperately they resist. Their bodies become their last citadel, which they are prepared to defend literally to the death. Yet, on the other side, of course, these people desperately need Mommy and Daddy, and are scared stiff of the very independence they are fighting to achieve.

Buechner wonders if the deepest truth about this particular sickness is not that two elemental cravings of the human spirit somehow come together in this disorder—the craving to be free and the craving to be taken care of and to be safe. By not eating, these people take their stand against a world that is telling them what to do. By not eating, they make their bodies much smaller, lighter and weaker, so that in effect, their bodies become like a child's body again and then the world flocks to their rescue.

Is something like this at the heart of this baffling disease? Buechner comes to a very poignant conclusion that I think has implications for every one of us. He says, "At least one thing is sure. By starving themselves, anorexics are speaking symbolically, and by trying above all else to make them start eating again, their families are in their own fashion speaking back the same way. Far beneath the issue of food there are, on both sides, unspoken issues of love, trust, fear, loss, separation. Father and mother, brother and sister, they are all of them afflicted together, acting out in pantomime a complex, subterranean drama whose nature they are at best only dimly aware of."

In response to this awesome human disorder, Buechner refers to some familiar words in the Epistle to the Ephesians where the author says, "Therefore, putting away falsehood, let everyone speak the truth with his neighbor, for we are members one of another." Here he gets to the heart of the issue, and perhaps to its final solution, I think. "If we would only speak the truth to one another—parents and children, friends and enemies, husbands and wives, strangers and lovers—we would no longer have to act out our deepest feelings in symbols that none of us understand. In our sickness, stubbornness, pride, we starve ourselves for what we hunger for above all else. 'Speaking the truth in love' is another phrase from Ephesians (4:15)," he ends up saying. "It is the only cure for the anorexia that afflicts us all."

As I have pondered this episode out of one troubled family system, it occurred to me that one of our greatest problems always in intimacy is our unwillingness or inability to share our deepest feelings, or to make clear what we need and want. There is an old notion that a person who loves another ought to be able to read the other's mind. I have had more than one spouse say to me, "If I have to ask him or her for it, that ruins the whole thing." But this is obviously not true to reality. We do not know the insides of another's mind and heart. Unless a person tells me what is going on in that inner citadel, I have no way of discerning that truth or shaping an appropriate response.

I had a good friend tell me once of something that had happened in her early childhood that only years later was she able to resolve effectively. This individual grew up in a farm family in southern Virginia, where there was very little physical affection shared between the parents and children. There was consistent and faithful caring for each other, but only rarely did they put their affection into words or loving gestures. When my friend was about ten, she went for the first time in her life to spend the night away from home, with her best friend from school. As the two little girls were preparing for bed, her friend's mother came in, tucked in both of the children and kissed each of them warmly on the cheek.

Such demonstrable affection was an absolute wonder to my friend, and immediately it evoked in her a desire for this same kind of thing from her own mother. So, she reported, the next night, back at home, when it was time for her to go to bed, she listened attentively as her mother came down the hall to do what she always did in the evening, which was to lay out a clean set of clothes for her daughter to wear to school the next day. With that, as usual, she said goodnight and closed the door. My friend reported that she had her cheek very prominently available for a kiss, and when there was no response of affection, she cried herself to sleep, concluding that her mother did not love her as much as her friend's mother loved her. The tragedy was that she did not tell her mother that night what she had experienced and what she so deeply wanted.

Twenty years went by, and by this time my friend had finished a graduate degree in social work and had been the beneficiary of a significant amount of personal therapy. On a visit back to the family farm, she and her mother were sitting one morning over the coffee cups at the breakfast table, and she emboldened herself to share the disappointment that she had felt that night twenty years before. When she related that experience, her mother began to cry softly and said, "I wish you had told me what you were feeling in that moment." She said, "You didn't realize it, but my mother died when I was very young and our father did the best he could to hold the family together. However, he wasn't able to do everything well and, as a result, not only did we not get any demonstrative affection, but many times, we had to go to school in dirty clothes."

She went on, "I made a resolve then and there that if I ever had children of my own, the way that I would show them my love was to see to it that they would always have clean clothes to wear to school." At that point, my friend began to cry also, because, you see, she had never understood the significance of that ritual of bringing in the school clothes any more than her mother had known the hunger of this little girl for physical affection. She said that they wound up embracing each other tenderly that morning, and grieved the fact that for thirty years they had been "ships in the night," missing an opportunity to meet each other's deepest needs because neither had been able to put into words what it was they most wanted and needed.

It is no wonder to me that, again and again in Holy Scripture, we are admonished to ask and to seek and to knock. The only way that others can learn how to love us realistically is if we give them a sense of who we are and what we want and need. It is this willingness to make ourselves known that sets the stage for a loving and appropriate response. Therefore, no matter how well you think you know another person or how clearly you think they ought to know you, the first law of authentic intimacy is telling our story honestly, making another aware of who we are and what we need. There is no guarantee that we will always get what we want, but to assume that because another person loves us, that one can read our minds, is a tragic mistake indeed. St. Paul wrote to the church in Philippi: "In everything, by prayer and supplication with thanksgiving, let your requests be made known." This is good counsel for all intimate relationships. In everything, keep on asking, keep on thanking, and above all keep on making yourself known. This provides the knowledge than enables love to know how to act.

[1] Frederick Buechner, *Whistling in the Dark* (San Francisco: Harper and Row, 1988).

Acceptance Is the Key

Luke 15:11-25

Well over a hundred years ago now, a Danish philosopher by the name of Søren Kierkegaard observed that sin is always at bottom a matter of mistaken identity. We humans act in destructive ways when we refuse to be who God created us to be. This can take the form of arrogance, in which we brashly attempt to be more than we are and overreach our appointed place, or it can go to the other extreme and take the form of apathy and irresponsibility, when we underreach and neglect the potentialities that are part of God's gift of creation.

The familiar story we call the parable of the Prodigal Son is an example of this issue of sin as an identity problem. At the outset of the story, the younger of the two sons could not accept the way life was given to him at his birth. He had grandiose images of his own importance and capabilities, which led him to look down on his father and his hometown and the whole surroundings of his life. This caused him to do a very heartless and arrogant thing—to walk in one day and say to his father, "Give me now my share of the inheritance." What he was really saying was, "I wish you were dead, old man, I wish you were no longer taking up space in my life. All I want is what you have. I wish this was the day after your funeral." Whether or not he realized the implications of his words, we do not know, but the interesting thing is that his father granted this brash request! Did he recognize perhaps that the kind of arrogance exhibited here could only be modified through the pain of actual experience? This lad was going to have to learn for himself what he refused to be taught by anyone else, and so he was allowed to set out on a fateful journey. Jesus says simply that he went to "a far country" and there it became quickly apparent that he was not as wise or as strong as he had deemed himself to be. He had undoubtedly embraced grandiose notions of his own competence and excellence. He may have even bragged to people before he left home as to how he was going to cover himself with glory when at last he had the freedom to act on his own. But, alas, what he discovered in the far country was the truth about himself—he was not the superman he had fantasized himself to be. In fact, what his father had been smart enough to make and save, he was dumb enough to squander and lose. In other words, the real world turned out to be far more complex and demanding than this naive young man had ever imagined, and he proceeded to have a head-on collision with things-as-they-are. His sense that he was better than everyone else in his family was thoroughly shattered.

But the story continues. A famine arose in this far country, and the lad had not used any of his inheritance to build friendships or create security. As a result, in abject poverty, he was forced to take a job on the lowest rung of the economic ladder. Here he was— a Jewish lad—reduced to having to tend and feed a herd of swine! It was a crushing blow to his inflated ego, but there in the vale of humiliation, something happened in the depths of his soul. He began to see how mistaken he had been to think himself so superior to his father or to home. Jesus says he began "to come to himself," to wake up from a stupor and start seeing reality as reality really exists.

However, as we humans so often do, having gone too far in one extreme, the lad proceeded to react and go too far in the other direction. He resolved to go back home, to acknowledge to his father his sin of arrogance, beg his forgiveness, and then ask if it would be possible for him to come back and live on the farm at the level of a tenant or a hired servant. He, who only a little while before had demanded total freedom, was now asking to have no freedom at all. He was so disillusioned with his own decision-making powers that he wanted now, in effect, to become a little child again. "Please, Daddy, take this terrible burden of freedom off of me," he seemed to be pleading. "Tell me when to get up and when to go to bed, when to turn this way and when to turn that way. Take me over completely. Let me climb back in the womb."

It is a predictable over-reaction to the collapse of grandiosity, and the wonderful thing about the story is that the old father, who had been wise enough to let the boy go and learn what he had to learn for himself, now refused to let him come home on the terms of becoming an infant again. Instead of saying, "Go get the bassinet, Daddy's little baby has come home and wants to stay dependant forever," the wise old man called for "a ring, a robe, and some shoes," emblems of authority and power and responsibility. By this action, he was saying: "While you are not a superman, neither are you a hired servant. You have the identity of a son in this family. We need you to help take responsibility for the family business. You do not have a right to think of yourself as better than any of the rest of us, nor must you sink to the level of thinking you are nothing but a slave." The father celebrated the growth that this lad had experienced in the far country in relation to his grandiosity and by giving him "a ring, a robe, and some shoes," he invited him to accept the identity that had been given him from the foundation of the world: to be who he was— no more, no less, but a child, a son, a responsible junior partner in the family.

Søren Kierkegaard was correct in suggesting that all our destructive behavior goes back to this issue of mistaken identity, this desire in us either to be more than we are, or to settle for being less. In a powerful novel entitled *The Prince of Tides*, Pat Conroy depicts a tragically flawed South Carolina family. The mother had grown up in great poverty and was an exceedingly beautiful woman. She had many gifts and opportunities that were open to her, but her one dream in life was being invited to join the Ladies League of the little town in which they lived. The social snobbery of that culture was such that no matter how beautiful she was, or how creatively she worked in the community, there was no chance of her being accepted by that particular group of women. And yet, this mother sacrificed everyone in her family in a desperate attempt to be something that really was not part of her created identity. As the children talked among themselves and wondered what drove her to make herself and everyone else so miserable, one of them concluded, "Mama always wants the one thing she can never get." This is the tragedy of trying to be more than one really can be.

The other extreme is also possible, however, and that is the willingness to settle for too little and under-utilize the real potential that God has planted in each of us. I still remember seeing parts of the trial of Adolf Eichmann after he had been tracked down in Argentina and brought before an Israeli court. They had him in a bullet-proof witness stand, for the feelings of hatred against him were so great. I was amazed at how innocuous he appeared. He was simply a bureaucrat in rimless glasses, the kind of man you would hardly notice if he sat next to you on a bus. However, this one had been the chief architect of "the final solution to the Jewish problem," which resulted in six million human beings losing their lives. When he was called to accountability for this monstrous crime against humanity, his only defense was to shrug his shoulders and say: "I could not help it. I was simply a cog in a machine. An order came down from above and I carried it out."

Yet the truth is he could have protested and resisted. We humans do not have total power, but we have some power, and when exercised faithfully and courageously, we can make a difference, as lives like

Winston Churchill's and Mahatma Ghandi's and Mother Teresa's so eloquently attest. Not to do what one could do can be just as lethal in its effect as the havoc caused by arrogance.

The real goal of Christian salvation is to help us come to terms both with our limits and the gifts that exist within the circle of our beings. This is how we live out authentically the gift of personhood that came to us at our birth. Accepting who and what I am, and not trying to be either more or less, is finally the secret above all secrets to human fulfillment.

Bob Benson gives a moving image of this ideal in his book *Laughter in the Walls*. It goes like this:

"One of our sons, Mike, wanted to take private speech lessons. He was such a talker anyway, I recommended 'hush' instead, but it was inexpensive, and he was interested, so we let him.

"The climax of the year's labor was a two-hour long assortment of clowns, kings, rabbits, and forgotten lines known as a Speech Recital, given to a devoted audience of eager parents and trapped friends. Mike was a king. He looked rather regal too, if I do say so myself. At least until the queen, a head taller and twenty pounds heavier, stood beside him casting a pall on his regality. He had only three lines to say— nine months of speech lessons—only three short lines—and they came very very late, in the last moment of the last act of the very last play. Any way you looked at it, he was not the star—at least not to anyone except a couple about halfway back on the left side. It was a long evening and it was miserably hot, but Mike waited and he was ready. In fact, he said his lines and he said them well. Not too soon, not too late, not too soft, but just right—*he said his lines!*

"I'm just a bit player, too, not a star in any way. But God gave me a line or so in the pageant of life, and when the curtain falls and the drama ends—and the stage is vacant at last—I don't ask for a critic's raves or fame in any amount. I only hope that I can hear him say, 'He said his lines, and he said them well, not too soon, not too late, not too loud, not too soft, but just right. *He said his lines!*'"

That is the high calling of God in Christ Jesus for us all.

Why or What

Job 38:1-7, 12, 16-18

Several years ago now, Rabbi Harold Kushner wrote a runaway best seller called *When Bad Things Happen to Good People*.[1] I saw him interviewed once on a television talk show and he said that if the book title had been *Why Bad Things Happen To Good People*, the volume would have been only one page long, and on that page would have been written three words: "I don't know." In other words, we humans always have a choice in the face of tragedy; we can approach the trauma by asking the speculative question, "*Why* has this happened?" or we can choose to ask the strategy question, "*What* do I do next now that this has occurred?"

There is a wonderful old story in the Bible about a man named Job, which spells out very dramatically the implications of these two approaches to life's tragedies. At the outset Job is described as being "blameless and upright," the greatest of all the individuals of the east. And then with shocking suddenness, the bottom falls out of every facet of his life. Some foreign raiders come in and steal most of his flocks and herds. All his children have gathered for a family celebration and a tornado strikes the house and wipes out all Job's heirs. Then his own health breaks down. He is rendered powerless and his body is covered with painful boils. And to make matters worse, his reputation is now shadowed by all this tragedy and real suspicions begin to form about the nature of his true character.

The remarkable thing is that Job somehow manages to cope with all these losses with a measure of grace and courage. In fact, he is able to keep his head above water until three of his friends come and proceed to turn this whole matter into one giant intellectual puzzle. Their concern is to find an explanation for all these events. They are intent on constructing some hypothesis to account for all these happenings. These so-called "comforters" embody the speculative approach to tragedy.

There was a widely accepted moral axiom in Job's day—that righteous behavior led to prosperity and evil behavior resulted in disaster. By this rule, it seemed obvious that Job must have done something awful to bring all this agony down upon his head. Therefore, these theoretical speculators wind up adding accusation to everything else that Job is having to face. "What terrible sin have you committed," they want to know, "that caused all these disasters?" Job finds their efforts to be utterly infuriating, and while he never claims that he is perfect, it is very clear to him that there is nothing he has ever done to justify this devastation. In fact, as the book unfolds, Job clearly gets the better of his accusers intellectually, but the problem is that their attempt to turn tragedy into a theoretical puzzle gets Job himself deflected from the path of practical coping, and he winds up going straight to God in stormy rage and demanding that the Almighty come down and give an account of what God has been doing and why. Job, in effect, wants to put the Ruler of the Universe on trial and get to the bottom intellectually of all that has taken place.

In the story, things get so overheated that God finally does come down to earth and appears to Job in a whirlwind. And yet, as Frederick Buechner has pointed out so effectively, God never does explain to Job why all these events occurred.[2] Buechner suggests at least two reasons for this approach. First of all, God could not explain it all to Job, because Job was a finite creature, and the reason why things happen ultimately resides in a depth of mystery that we humans do not have the capacities to plumb. In the text at the outset of this chapter, God asks Job: "Where were you when I laid the foundations of the earth? Have you commanded the morning since your days began, or caused the dawn to know its place? Have you entered into the springs of the sea or walked into the recesses of the deep?" In other words, Job did not begin to have the intellectual capacities to fathom all the realities behind our complex universe. Buechner says explaining these events to Job would be about as futile as trying to explain Einstein's theory of relativity to a small-neck crab! The immensity of the one is utterly beyond the capacity of the other. We humans cannot fully understand why things happen because we are finite by nature and not the ultimate Creator of all things.

Buechner goes on to say that the second reason why God offers Job no explanation is that this really was not what he most needed in that moment. Even if God could have put all the facts on a chart on the wall and been able to answer satisfactorily all the questions that these events might have raised, Job would have still faced the challenge of having to live with the empty chairs at the breakfast room table! The point is that in the depths of our tragic experiences what we need most is the courage to face a world made radically different by what has happened and the strength somehow to stoop over and pick up the pieces and see what we can make of what is left. Courage and hope are more valuable than a thousand intellectual answers. Therefore, God does not give Job simply a theoretical explanation; he comes and offers Job the gift of his own presence and the promise that in the midst of all this God would be with Job and for Job, and that would be enough. In the final analysis, God's companionship, not some theoretical explanation, was the resource offered Job by the Ultimate and Holy One.

I find this to be utterly relevant to those times in my life when the bottom has suddenly dropped out and I am faced with a radically different situation than I knew in the past. To center in on the fact that I am still breathing and to interpret that to mean that God still wants me to be upon this earth and still has meaning to give my life—that is of more practical value than all the abstract answers in the world. If we can just remember that life is gift, that we came into this world initially not because we earned it or deserved it but because the Mysterious and Generous One wanted us to be, that will help. Then perhaps we can realize that what birth is to our beginnings, breath is to our present condition. Listen, the One who wanted us to be originally is still giving us life, and with that One, *there is no abandonment*! As long as I am still breathing, I can embrace the hope that God still wants me to be, and from that I can conclude that the One who gave me "the good old days" so graciously can be trusted to give me good new days as well. The God of our birth and breath is our hope for a meaningful future. He said to Job what Jesus would say to his disciples centuries later, "Lo, I am with you always! Therefore, be not afraid." This is where we get the strength to ask the strategy question, "*What* do I do next?". Rather than spending all my energies on the speculative question, "*Why*?", I can begin to sift through the wreckage, pick up the pieces and see what can be made of what is left: not because I understand it all but because my very breath is a sign to me that I am still companioned by the Lord of life. That One still wants me to be; therefore I have a future in spite of all the losses of the past. Buechner says that when this gift of companionship came clear to Job, everything began to look differently. He was like a man "who asked for a crust and wound up being given the whole loaf." It is a possibility open to every one of us in the deepest and darkest places of our lives.

You are still breathing, aren't you? For that reason, if for no other, take hope, my friend, take hope!

[1] Harold S. Kushner, *When Bad Things Happen to Good People* (New York: Schocken Books, 1981).

[2] Frederick Buechner, *Wishful Thinking: a theological ABC* (New York: Harper and Row, 1973).

The Communion of Saints

Revelation 7:9-17

Several years ago now, I got a glimpse into the meaning of that special day in the Christian year called All Saints' Day, when we pause to remember the unnumbered host of human beings who have lived and died before us and make up the great heritage of our own lives. The episode which shed this light was something that happened to the renowned naturalist and anthropologist, Dr. Loren Eiseley.

It seems that he had been commissioned by a zoo in a large European city to secure certain birds and reptiles in the Colorado Rockies. One spring night, he and his helpers made their way into a mountain valley and found there an abandoned cabin of stone that had been built in the land rush days, but subsequently left because the soil had not been able to support any farming. Dr. Eiseley had learned before that buildings such as these were wonderful places to capture wild birds. Since these structures were going back to nature themselves, their unoccupied reaches were a perfect setting for birds to nest.

Dr. Eiseley describes how he opened the door very softly and had his spotlight ready to turn on and blind whatever birds might be sleeping under those eaves. He placed a ladder carefully against the far wall where there was a shelf, and as he began to climb up, he heard a bird or two stir their wings, but nothing flew into the faint starlight through the many holes in the roof. He quietly slithered up the ladder until his head and arms were over the shelf. Then he turned on his blinding flashlight and reached over the ledge to seize whatever was there. Everything worked perfectly, he said, except for one detail; he did not realize the kind of bird he was going to encounter there. Here is what he wrote later:

"I snapped on the flash and sure enough there was a great beating and feathers flying, but instead of my having them, they, or rather he, had me. He had my hand, that is, and for a small hawk not much bigger than my fist he was doing all right. I heard him give one short metallic cry when the light went on and my hand descended on the bird beside him; after that he was busy with his claws and his beak was sunk in my thumb. In the struggle I knocked the lamp over on the shelf, and his mate got her sight back and whisked neatly through the hole in the roof and off among the stars outside. It all happened in fifteen seconds and you might think I would have fallen down the ladder, but no, I had a professional . . . reputation to keep up. . . .[The bird] chewed my thumb up pretty effectively and lacerated my hand with his claws, but in the end I got him, having two hands to work with.

"He was a sparrow hawk and a fine young male in the prime of life. I was sorry not to catch the pair of them, but as I dripped blood and folded his wings carefully, holding him by the back so he couldn't strike again, I had to admit the two of them might have been more than I could have handled under the circumstances. The little fellow had saved his mate by diverting me, and that was that. He was born to it, and made no outcry now, resting in my hand hopelessly, but peering toward me in the shadows behind the lamp with a fierce, almost indifferent glance. He neither gave nor expected mercy and something out of the high air passed from him to me, stirring a faint embarrassment. I quit looking into that eye and managed to get my huge carcass with its fist full of prey back down the ladder. I put the bird in a box too small to allow him to injure himself by struggle and walked out to welcome [my other companions]. It had been a long day, and camp still to make in the darkness. In the morning that bird would be just another episode. He would go back . . . in [a] truck to a small cage in a city where he would spend the rest of his life. And a good thing, too. I sucked my aching thumb and spat out some blood . . .

"In the morning, with the change that comes on suddenly in that high country, the mist that had hovered below us in the valley was gone. The sky was a deep blue, and one could see for miles over the high outcroppings of stone. I was up early and brought the box in which the little hawk was imprisoned out onto the grass where I was building a cage. A wind as cool as a mountain spring ran over the grass and stirred my hair. It was a fine day to be alive. I looked up and all around and at the hole in the cabin roof out of which the other little hawk had fled. There was no sign of her anywhere that I could see. 'Probably in the next county by now,' I thought cynically, but before beginning work I decided I'd have a look at my last night's capture . . . I got him right out in my hand with his wings folded properly and I was careful not to startle him. He lay limp in my grasp and I could feel his heart pound under the feathers but he only looked beyond me and up. I saw him look that last look away beyond me into a sky so full of light that I could not follow his gaze. The little breeze flowed over me again, and nearby a mountain aspen shook all its tiny leaves. I suppose I must have had an idea then of what I was going to do, but I never let it come up into consciousness. I just reached over and laid the hawk on the grass. He lay there a long minute without hope, unmoving, his eyes still fixed on that blue vault above him. It must have been that he was already so far away in heart that he never felt the release from my hand. He never even stood. He just lay with his breast against the grass.

"In the next second after that long minute he was gone. Like a flicker of light, he had vanished with my eyes full on him, but without actually seeing even [the way his wings began to] beat. He was gone straight into that towering emptiness of light and crystal that my eyes could scarcely bear to penetrate. For another long moment there was silence. I could not see him. The light was too intense. Then from far up some- where a cry came ringing down. I was young then and had seen little of the world, but when I heard that cry my heart turned over. It was not the cry of the hawk I had captured; for, by shifting my position against the sun, I was now seeing further up. Straight out of the sun's eye, where she must have been soaring restlessly above us for untold hours, hurtled his mate. And from far up, ringing from peak to peak of the summits over us, came a cry of such unutterable and ecstatic joy that it sounds down across the years and tingles among the cups on my quiet breakfast table. I saw them both now. He was rising fast to meet her. They met in a great soaring gyre that turned into a whirling circle and a dance of wings. Once more, just once, their two voices, joined in a harsh wild medley of question and response, struck and echoed against the pinnacles of the valley. Then they were gone forever somewhere into those upper regions beyond the eyes of men."

That image of one loving creature rushing to meet another is as fine a picture of ultimate Christian hope as anything I know. What we believe about what lies beyond the grave grows out of our conviction that God's love for us humans is larger than life and stronger than death. When the Eternal One called each of us out of nothing into being, it was not a careless or irresponsible act, but rather the beginning of a process that God wants to go on forever. And the relationships of love which we begin to form during our earthly pilgrimages have implications far beyond our "three score and ten years" in history. The image of one beloved creature welcoming the ascent of another is a profound image of how the great community of the dead will respond to each new traveler that makes his or her way into the next stage of God's Great Adventure. That some kind of joyful meeting will occur, which builds on the memory of past love

but promises to grow even more fully into the future—
that is the hope that comes to those who see reality
through the lens of the Christian gospel. None of us
knows in precise detail what it is like to die, and yet,
Eiseley's picture of two tiny creatures, bonded in life,
and therefore ecstatically joyful to be reunited after
separation, gives deep insight to me into the nature
of love and also the prospects of hope.

Three summers ago, I heard Fred Craddock of
the Candler School of Divinity of Emory University in
Atlanta preach a moving communion of saints' sermon using the whole sixteenth chapter of Romans as
his text. As you may know, this is largely a listing of
names. St. Paul is writing to the church in Rome and
asking to be remembered to a variety of individuals
whose lives have become linked to his somewhere in
the past. Dr. Craddock invited all of us in that service
to get out our bulletins and begin to write our list of
beloved individuals. He instructed us to carry that
list with us wherever we went in the future and to add
names to it as the circle of our affection grew. He went
so far as to say, "When you die, take that list with you
into the next life." Then he said, "I know when you get
to Heaven's Gate, St. Peter will stop you and say,
'Look, you can't bring anything with you from the
other life. Let me have that piece of paper.' And you
will probably say, 'Oh, it's really not anything. It's
just a list of people whom I have loved and who have
loved me across the years.' And St. Peter will say, 'Can
I look at it?' And you will stand on one foot and then
the other and say, 'Oh, these names wouldn't mean
any more to you than the names St. Paul wrote in his

letter to the Romans. They are just my particular communion of saints.' But St. Peter will insist, and you will finally hand over the list to him," said Dr. Craddock. Then he concluded by saying: "St. Peter will take that list and begin to read it: 'Frank, Susan, George, Bill, Ophelia,' and then a great smile will break across his face, and he will say, 'Do you know what? When I was walking over to work this afternoon, I saw these very people. They were making a poster. It had your name on it, and it said, *Welcome Home!*' "

Again, this is the hope we have, because the Love that birthed us in the beginning is larger than life and stronger than death. And once we begin to love each other, because of God, there will be no end to it. Blessed be God. Blessed be he! Amen.

[1] Loren Eiseley, *The Immense Journey* (New York: Random House).

First Class—Jesus Style

Luke 22:24-27

Several years ago, my family and I lived for a period in west Texas, and during that time, we learned an interesting fact about the kind of travel that was common-place there in the nineteenth century. Stage-coaches were the principal means of getting from one place to the other in that vast wild territory. What I had never heard before was that there were three classes of tickets on a stagecoach, just as today on a modern airline there are first-class and tourist-class accommodations. In stagecoach practice, however, these different levels had nothing to do with where in the vehicle you sat, or how much room you had or the kind of food you were served. They pertained rather to what was expected of you in a time of crisis. You see, given the poor quality of the roadways back then, on many occasions a vehicle would get bogged down in the mud or come to an incline so steep that the horses would be unable to climb it.

It was in those moments that the kind of ticket you had bought took on significance. For example, a first-class ticket entitled you to stay in the stage-coach, no matter what the circumstances. This was the most expensive, and correspondingly asked the least of you in a situation of difficulty. A second-class passenger was required to get out and walk around the mud-bog or trudge up the hill on foot to lighten the load. It was the third-class passenger, the one who had the least status, who was required to help the driver either push the vehicle through the mud or help the horses get it up the hill. Those who paid the most had to do the least, and those who paid the least had the most asked of them.

As I heard this little snippet of nineteenth century lore, it struck me how different this was from the hierarchy of values that Jesus of Nazareth left for his disciples twenty centuries ago. In the text at the beginning of this chapter, an argument had broken out among Jesus' followers about the issue of who would be the greatest in the coming kingdom. They were debating this whole matter of what constitutes first-class and second-class and third-class standing among their peers. Jesus pointed out that the culture in which they lived was very clear at this point. The Gentiles made first-class status a matter of privilege. They were the ones who lorded it over others and made them do whatever it was that they wanted. But Jesus said, "I am turning that world of values upside down. I say to you, the really first-class citizen in this world is the one who is willing to serve; the person who is quick to climb down and get his feet in the mud and his hands in the dirt and to do whatever needs to be done in order for the common good to be advanced. This is what I designate as the highest in the order of reality." You see, for Jesus, servanthood was not an emblem of shame at all, but represented the highest status to which a human being could aspire.

This was not a tangential issue in Jesus' thinking, but a central concern. On the last night of his life, as he gathered his disciples for a final meal, he acted out this same revolutionary principle. The twelve were still smarting from their argument over who was going to be first and who was going to be last, and as a result, none of them was in a mood to do the lowly task of washing the feet of the others so they could eat their meal in comfort. Sensing their competitiveness, Jesus stood up from the table, laid aside his own clothing, wrapped himself in the garb of a slave, and proceeded to wash the feet of all the disciples. He was not above the menial task of dealing with the dirt! It needed to be done if they were to get on with the rest of the evening, and he demonstrated here a willingness to do it. This is what it means to be a real servant, and Jesus said this constitutes the very pinnacle of human greatness. In the Christian sense, this reality is not defined by the privilege that exempts one from hardship, but rather by the earthy willingness to do whatever needs to be done so the common good is served.

It is obvious that after twenty centuries, we have still not fully grasped this insight that Jesus both taught and embodied. And yet, for those who have eyes to see, there is evidence all around that such servanthood is what makes the world go around and is the most valuable quality that any human being can bring to a situation.

Langdon Gilkey was teaching at a private school in interior China in 1943 when the Japanese took over the mainland. He was one of fifteen hundred Allied citizens who were rounded up and put in a prisoner of war camp called Shantung Compound. Many of these American and Canadian and British and Dutch citizens had gone to China on some kind of missionary or humanitarian endeavor. However, Gilkey was amazed at how inhumane they became with each other when the food supply got scarce and the living space cramped. He was familiar with the concept that "perfect love casts out fear," but what he saw developing before his eyes was the process of fear casting out love. He witnessed how the insecurity of that situation turned erstwhile missionaries into vicious competitors, individuals who were willing to stoop to anything in order to secure their own survival. Any notion of the common good evaporated completely.

The one exception in all that prison camp was a group of Dutch Benedictine monks whose monastery had been overrun by the Japanese. These individuals had long before made a commitment to simplicity and servanthood, and Gilkey watched with wonder as these folk quietly set about to do whatever needed to be done in simple service while everyone else in their fearfulness was caught up in exploitation. He saw under those dramatic human circumstances that the most valuable quality of all was not how much a person knew intellectually, or the rank they held socially, but how willing they were to become a genuine servant!

This same truth was echoed in a series of television interviews that Bill Moyers did with Joseph Campbell just before the death of this renowned scholar. Joseph Campbell had lived deeply into the many cultures on our planet and perhaps knew more than any other living soul about those ancient stories that make up the heritage of our world. He said at one point that the ultimate aim of all human quests for authenticity was neither a release from pain nor ecstasy for oneself, but the wisdom and the power to serve others. He said the final distinction between a celebrity and a hero is that the former lives only for himself, while the latter makes his ultimate aim the redemption of human society.

As I heard this renowned scholar reflect the best wisdom from all the cultures, I realized that Jesus was at the heart of reality itself when he said, "Let the one who would be greatest among you be the one who serves." On nineteenth century stagecoaches, first-class travel was defined in terms of the privilege of not having to do something in a time of need. In Jesus' understanding of reality, the first-class way to live in our kind of world is precisely the opposite. It is the willingness to get out and push the vehicle for the common good through whatever it might be facing. Here is the finest expression of what it means to be fully human. The greatest finally are not those who exempt themselves from effort, but those who are willing to serve.

And this, dear friend, is within the reach of every one of us. You do not have to have a Ph.D. in order to be a serving person. Everyone has access to this kind of first-class status.

Light and Warmth

Mark 1:9-10

Johann Wolfgang Goethe was the last of the so-called "universal men." This means that he had developed a mastery of virtually every area of human competence. He was at once a playwright, a historian, a scientist, and a musician. There was hardly any subject about which his knowledge was not extraordinary. One of his biographers tells that as he lay dying in 1832, he suddenly sat bolt upright in bed and cried, "Light, light, more light." These turned out to be his very last words, for he fell back and died moments later. The biographer said that this was a fitting climax to this particular individual's human drama. His whole life had been devoted to acquiring more and more light, pushing the parameters of darkness further and further back. Many years later the Spanish philosopher, Miguel Unamuno, was reading this particular biography, and the story is that when he came to the deathbed scene, he closed the book and said to his wife, "For all of his brilliance, Goethe was finally mistaken. Instead of crying 'Light, light, more light,' what he should have cried for was, 'Warmth, warmth, more warmth,' for we humans do not die of the darkness, we die of the cold."

I was very intrigued when I first read of this exchange between these two giants of our western civilization. However, as I have reflected on the matter, it seems to me that in one sense each of them was right and wrong at the same time. For example, I do not agree with Unamuno's assertion that "we humans do not die of the darkness." I would argue that knowledge and wisdom are utterly indispensable in our becoming human and remaining human. I would even go so far as to say that again and again in life, a lack of knowledge is a disastrous condition.

Many years ago, when I was serving a parish in Kentucky, I got in the mail one day a packet that contained a little paperback book entitled *On Understanding Woman* and one of the most poignant letters I ever read. It seems that years before an older couple in the northern part of that state had given birth to a little girl after years of trying and almost concluding that they would never have the privilege of having a child. By this time, they were relatively affluent and able to give this long-awaited one every advantage that money could buy. She went to the best of private schools, dressed in the finest of clothes, and was accorded every privilege of which they could think. Imagine, then, her parent's dismay, when one day after her thirteenth birthday, she got one of her father's hunting rifles, locked herself in her room, put the barrel in her mouth and took her own life!

In the days that followed her funeral, they were going through her personal effects and found a diary she had been keeping, and only then discovered that for all the things they had given her, they had failed to prepare her properly for the stage of life into which she was moving. Like any child growing into adolescence, things were happening to her body and to her relationships with others that she did not understand. Because the overly privileged are often unaccustomed to discomfort, this child, in panic, chose the abrupt exit of suicide. The letter concluded: "We have decided to take the money that we had put aside for our daughter's college education and use it to provide every clergy person in Kentucky with a copy of the enclosed book. If we had known the truths that it contains and had been able to communicate these to our little daughter, the chances are she would be alive and with us today."

When I put that letter down, I felt that profound hush that comes over one's soul in the face of the awesome. And from somewhere, the words that Jesus prayed from the cross came to my mind: "Father, forgive them, for they know not what they do." So much of the anguish that we experience does not derive from human badness, but from human blindness. What we don't know most assuredly can hurt us! Therefore, I do not agree with Unamuno that warmth is the only thing our species needs. People like this little girl in Kentucky do die of the darkness. Our need to know is very profound and essential indeed.

However, Unamuno did have a point nonetheless, which is that one can possess all the knowledge in the world, but if there is not that energy and vitality which we associate with warmth, existence does tend to freeze over and not grow into the grand thing that it was meant to be. In addition to knowing the shape of reality, I also need contact with the power which will enable me to act on that vision and embody those ideals. St. Paul claimed that this was the crux of his own agony before he encountered the risen Christ: "The good that I would, I do not," he wrote, and "the evil that I would not, that I do. The will to do right was present in me, but not the power to do it." He was pointing here to the need for vibrancy as well as vision. We all *know* better than we *do*, which is why the cry "Warmth, warmth, more warmth" really does have validity.

Corrie Ten Boom was one of many Christians in the 1930s and 40s who could not in good conscience see what the Germans were doing to her Jewish neighbors and do nothing about it. Therefore, her family home just outside Amsterdam became a hiding place for several Dutch Jewish folk. They were eventually caught in this covert action and sent along with their Jewish friends to one of those terrible concentration camps of eastern Europe. The degradation of that experience was too much for Miss Ten Boom's beloved older sister and she died while incarcerated. Corrie Ten Boom herself managed to survive, and after the war became known all over Europe for her clarion call that divine forgiveness was the only hope to heal the wounds of the past and make for a different future.

She wrote that years later she was in Bavaria giving a talk on the importance of forgiveness to a church group there. As the congregation was filing out, a tall German man came up with tears in his eyes and said, "I needed to hear what you said tonight, perhaps more than anybody else on this earth." Miss Ten Boom froze in her tracks, because she suddenly recognized this man as one of the guards in the prison camp who had been particularly inhumane in his treatment of her and her sister and all the inmates there. Suddenly all the idealism about forgiveness vanished from her heart. She realized in that moment she was incapable of doing what in her head she knew was right and what she had just advocated for all Europe. She reports that in that moment she had no other recourse except to ask for "warmth, warmth, more warmth"; that is, she had to ask God for the energy to act on the vision she had just articulated. And she claims that from some far reach of the universe, from a place deep in the heart of the Holy One, there came a power to lift her arm, extend her hand, and lovingly touch a man who a few years before had blatantly abused her. The strength to do that, she claimed, came from somewhere else. It is not enough to know what we should do. We also stand in need of being given the power to do it.

The wonderful thing about the Christian gospel is that in the person of Jesus Christ both our need for light and our need for warmth have been abundantly supplied by our redeeming God. When Jesus was ready to begin his adult ministry, he went himself to the place where John the Baptist was preparing the way and was immersed in the waters of the Jordan River, thus identifying totally with the people he came to save. As he came up out of the water, a great light shone upon him, as well as incredible warmth from the heart of God. Then he heard those utterly affirming words: "This is my beloved son, in whom I am well pleased." That was the beginning of the light of God and the warmth of God pouring through this One into the human situation.

All of this means that God provides us everything that our species needs, not just some of the things. Jesus said, "I am the way, the truth, and the life." I take that to mean that his way embraces both the truth that we need to know and the life and energy that we need to do it. In the person of Jesus Christ, "light, light, more light" and "warmth, warmth, more warmth" come together, and this turns out to be the secret of our salvation. Here is precisely what we need to become all we were meant to be, and when you finally see it and begin to experience it, it makes you want to say, "At last! At last! Hallelujah!"

Gratitude and Ambiguity

John 6:1-14

As another Thanksgiving Day looms near, you will undoubtedly hear again an account of how this national holiday came into existence. The story begins well over a year before the actual event. In the summer of 1620, a sizeable group of adventuresome citizens set out in two ships from Southampton, England, with the intention of establishing a colony in the Virginia territory of the New World. As they sailed around the southern tip of the British Isles, however, one of the boats called the Speedwell proved unseaworthy, and so they were forced to pull in at Plymouth and some of the people gave up. Those who still wanted to make the journey crowded onto a ship called the Mayflower and set out to sea once again.

The trip took much longer than they had anticipated—sixty-six days, actually—and, since their instruments for navigation were very primitive, unbeknownst to them they were blown hundreds of miles off course. When they finally sighted land, it was not Virginia at all but what we now call New England. They had hoped to arrive in time to build shelters before the winter set in, but it was almost December by now. They sent scouting parties ashore. They were able with great difficulty to construct shelters of a sort, but they were inadequate against the brutal elements of that region.

Overexposure led to disease of all kinds, and before the spring finally came exactly half of the one hundred and two people who had set out from Plymouth were buried in unmarked graves, for they did not want the Indians to know how decimated their ranks had become. There was not a family in the community that did not lose at least one of its own during that terrible winter seige. When spring did come, what was left of the crew of the Mayflower prepared to return to England, for it was a rented ship, and a spirited discussion took place as to whether the whole project should not be abandoned and the survivors go back with them. However, in a gesture of real courage and hope, they decided to stay on. With the help of some friendly Indians, they planted about thirty acres of grain. They were able to build more substantial shelters for themselves and, come fall, the harvest was more abundant than anything they had ever known in the old country.

As the time for the first anniversary of their landing came in view, a discussion arose as to how they should commemorate this occasion. The first suggestion was that they make it a day of mourning. After all, the losses during this first year had been staggering, and a time of focusing on the honored dead seemed to be in order. However, another suggestion was put forth, that it should be a day of thanksgiving. Even though they had lost a great deal, it was argued there was also much room for gratitude. After

all, they had survived, the Indians had been unex-
pectedly hospitable, and the land had proved to be
fertile beyond their wildest imagination. Why not
focus on thanksgiving, rather than mourning? The
story is that the debate moved back and forth between these two alternatives, and as you know from
subsequent history, the thanksgiving party won out!

I would like to suggest that this one decision may
have had as much to do with the future development
of our country as any other one thing. I say this
because in every situation of ambiguity—that is,
when we are faced with many alternatives—we always have a choice. On the one hand, we can choose
to focus on what we have lost and all the hardships
we have experienced, and the combination of the
forces that are going against us. Or, we can choose to
focus on the things that are going for us, the things we
have to celebrate, those realities that are energizing
us rather than diminishing us. In every situation of
ambiguity, both possibilities are present, and I am
contending that what our forefathers chose in making their first anniversary a day of thanksgiving
rather than a day of mourning was a crucial factor in
the way they proceeded to negotiate all the other
challenges they had to face in those early years. And
as we face another Thanksgiving season, we would do
well to remind ourselves that what was true for them
is true for us as well, that in every situation, we too
have a choice, and of all these the wisest by far is the
choice of gratitude.

I remember quite well when I got my first inkling
of this important truth. I could not have been over six

years old. I had the great good fortune of having a Sunday school teacher who knew how to communicate with children in terms of objects rather than concepts. On the Sunday before Thanksgiving that year, we entered her classroom and saw a large glass container on the table, partially filled with a red colored liquid. As the class began, the teacher invited us to engage this substance with all our senses. We were allowed to smell it, and taste it, and lift it up to the light to see its color, and feel how heavy it was. Then after getting us thoroughly involved in this kind of exploration, she asked, "Can someone tell me: is this container half-full or half-empty?" A little girl in the class, who always tended to negativity, was the first to speak. She said loudly, "It's half-empty, it's half empty." Another little boy, who had the makings of a philosopher, responded promptly, "No, it's not, it's half-full," and back and forth the discussion went. I will never forget that after a while the teacher said, "You know, the truth is that technically you are both right. It is half-empty; it is also half-full. But it makes all the difference in the world which way you choose to look at it. If you focus on the half-emptiness, chances are you are going to feel discouraged. You will wish that there were more, and wind up feeling negatively about the whole thing. On the other hand, if you focus on what is there, on the half-fullness— that will give you something for which to be grateful, a delight and sense of satisfaction about the way things are. I hope you will choose to focus on the half-fullness."

I have never forgotten that lesson. Both descriptions were true, but there is more to be gained humanly from siding with what is going with you than in focusing on what is going against you. It has been over fifty years since I had that experience, but I have yet to come across anything that denies its basic truth.

For example, I remember years ago visiting a large hospital and calling on two parishioners of mine who were patients there. Both of them were women in their middle eighties, and each was up against an enormous array of physical difficulties. When I entered the first lady's room, I immediately sensed that she was badly depressed by her situation and she lost little time in cataloguing her complaints to me. She told me how she loathed having to leave the familiarity of her home and come to a hospital, and how it was impossible to get any sleep there because of all the interruptions day and night. She reported that the sheets on the bed were just like sandpaper, and perhaps the worst thing of all was the terrible food that the hospital provided. There was not a thing about her complaints that was not true. I did my best to remind her of God's presence with her, and even offered a prayer for her encouragement, but as I left, the atmosphere was still heavy with depression, and I found myself drained by the whole encounter.

Two floors down, I entered the room of another woman, herself aged and up against it, but I could tell from the moment I opened the door that there was a different atmosphere in that place. When I told her how sorry I was that she had to come to the hospital, she said, "Well, I'm sorry too that I have this problem, but you know, there are things that the people here can do for me that my family at home could not do. I'm grateful that places like this exist." I asked: "Do you find the commotion of the hospital disturbing to your rest?" She said, "You know, the truth is, my family at home is wonderful to me, but they have their work to do, which means I often get quite lonely. I frankly enjoy all the human contact that a hospital provides. Every time the door opens, I find myself wondering what fresh young thing is coming in now." "Do you find the bed difficult to sleep on?" I asked, remembering the complaint that I had heard moments before. With that her eyes brightened, and she said, "We only change our sheets at home once a week. They change them here every day! I call that real luxury, don't you?" I remember making one other effort at consolation. "Do you find the food here hard to eat?" Again, she said, "You know, my daughter-in-law is a wonderful cook, but she tends to fix things the same way all the time, and it gets a little boring. I really enjoy the variety of the menu here." And then she added: "Eating for me under any circumstances is not easy, because I only have two teeth left. But I thank the Lord, *they hit!"*

When she made that last statement, I felt like stepping back and giving her a full military salute. All the heroism in the world is not confined to the battle-field. Here was a person who was really up against it, but she had chosen to focus on the half-fullness, rather than the half-emptiness, and the difference in the energy level in those two hospital rooms was absolutely amazing.

Therefore, I come back to saying that the decision that lies behind our national holiday of Thanksgiving is a reminder of something very basic to reality. In every situation of ambiguity, there are things to lament and things to celebrate, things going for us and things going against us. In those moments, the wisest choice any of us can make is to align with the positive against the negative. Isn't that exactly what we see Jesus doing in the text at the beginning of this chapter? As that hungry multitude was growing restless, the disciples said, "We've got to do something to avoid a crisis. Let the people go before they turn on us." All they could see was the half-emptiness in that lonely place. But Jesus surprised them by asking: "What resources do we have? Let's look at the half-fullness, and find out what we have to be thankful for, rather than to be fearful of." And when it turned out that there was a lad there with five loaves and two fishes, what did Jesus do? He took what was there and gave thanks for it and that became enough! It is everlastingly true that in the situations of ambiguity, we always have a choice! Our forebears modeled for us the way to cope with ambiguity. May this Thanksgiving find us not only grateful but wiser because of what they did.